Civic Skills and Values

Self-Control

By Dalton Rains

www.littlebluehousebooks.com

Copyright © 2024 by Little Blue House, Mendota Heights, MN 55120. All rights reserved. No part of this book may be reproduced or utilized in any form or by any means without written permission from the publisher.

Little Blue House is distributed by North Star Editions:
sales@northstareditions.com | 888-417-0195

Produced for Little Blue House by Red Line Editorial.

Photographs ©: iStockphoto, cover, 9; Shutterstock Images, 4, 7, 11, 12, 15, 17, 18, 20–21, 23, 24 (top left), 24 (top right), 24 (bottom left), 24 (bottom right)

Library of Congress Control Number: 2022919908

ISBN
978-1-64619-821-4 (hardcover)
978-1-64619-850-4 (paperback)
978-1-64619-906-8 (ebook pdf)
978-1-64619-879-5 (hosted ebook)

Printed in the United States of America
Mankato, MN
082023

About the Author

Dalton Rains writes and edits nonfiction children's books. He lives in Minnesota.

Table of Contents

Good Choices **5**

Struggles **13**

Why It Matters **19**

Glossary **24**

Index **24**

Good Choices

Self-control means you think before you act.

Then you are able to make good choices.

Self-control is important at school. You might know the answer to a question. Instead of yelling it, you raise your hand.

You can use self-control on Halloween.

You might want to eat all your candy right away.

But it will last longer if you eat a little at a time.

In the car, self-control can be helpful.
You sit still and wait until you get home.

Struggles

Self-control can be hard.

You want to open your present right away.

But you have to wait until the holiday.

You might feel tired. You might not have much energy to do your homework.

Rewards can help.
Give yourself a short
break after finishing a
hard problem.
Self-control can help you
do good work.

Why It Matters

Self-control is good for you
and for others.

When you stay quiet during a
movie, everyone can watch
and listen.

You wait in the lunch line at school.

You do not cut in line or push others.

Everyone gets a turn.

Self-control can be hard,
but it is important.
It helps you work hard
and be kind to others.

Glossary

candy

movie

Halloween

present

Index

C
car, 10

H
homework, 14

P
problem, 16

S
school, 6, 20